Each of us is limitless; each of us with his or her right upon the earth.

– Walt Whitman

This above all: to thine ownself be true.

\- Shakespeare

Excellence is not an act, but a habit.

– Aristotle

No act of kindness, no matter how small, is ever wasted.

– Aesop

The way to be happy is to make others so.

– Robert Ingersoll

Be happy for this moment. This moment is your life.

– Omar Kayyam

Peace is always beautiful.

- Walt Whitman

The greatest mistake you can make in life is to be continually fearing you will make one.

– Elbert Hubbard

Bloom where you are planted.

- 1 Corinthians KJV

Made in the USA
Coppell, TX
15 December 2023

26298030R00056